'Last Night A Bidet Drenched My Wife'

Words by @trouteyes

ILLUSTRATIONS BY MOOSE ALLAIN

'Last Night A Bidet Drenched My Wife'

...and other misheard lyrics

BLINK
bringing you closer

Published by Blink Publishing
The Plaza,
535 Kings Road,
Chelsea Harbour,
London, SW10 0SZ

www.blinkpublishing.co.uk

facebook.com/blinkpublishing
twitter.com/blinkpublishing

Hardback – 978-1-7-8870-212-6
Ebook – 978-1-7-8870-213-3

A CIP catalogue of this book is available from the British Library.

Typeset by EnvyDesign Ltd
Printed and bound in Great Britain by Clays Ltd, Elcograf S.p.A.

1 3 5 7 9 10 8 6 4 2

© @trouteyes 2019

Blink Publishing is an imprint of Bonnier Books UK
www.bonnierbooks.co.uk

I don't have to tell you I'm sure you understand
The first who lay beside me
Made me what I am, oh you made me what I am
And no matter how it ends
You should always keep in touch with your friends

– The Wedding Present

Introduction

Hello. How's it gonig? Hope you are all donig well.

Thanks so much for parting with your hard-earned cash to buy this piece of tomfoolery, lovingly assembled by myself and the wonderful @MooseAllain. I would like to express an enormous al fresco fungrunt to the many good people of twitter.com who have been so supportive of @trouteyes for the last ten years – you know who you are. I really do appreciate your kindness.

For those of you who don't know, twitter.com started when Ceefax and Club Penguin merged in 1929 and took over Friends Reunited. It wasn't until much later that I joined, and to start with, I had no idea what to 'tweet'. I didn't have anything remotely useful to say. The whole idea seemed like hashtag bullshit to me. What was it for? Should I talk about my day? Tell everyone about my real life? Not a chance. Too shy shy, hush hush gammy eye.

Luckily, someone who knew how twitter.com worked pointed me in the direction of a few funny accounts who understood how to do it properly and the penny dropped – I COULD SAY ABSOLUTELY ANYTHING AT ALL. It didn't have to be true, in fact it was way better if it wasn't. Excellent.

The floodgates opened and the innermost thoughts of my foolish noggin spilled out into the internet and slopped around all of its various sections. *I was off.* I loved the anonymity of @trouteyes. He was able to bang out all kinds of babble that I couldn't say in the real world, which felt terrifically liberating. Self-publishing 140 characters of garbage whenever the mood took me. I was gripped.

Look at me Kenny, I'm microblogging! It became a big electronic notebook of nonsense and most lovely of all, slowly, slowly, people began to like it.

Anything could spark a tweet: a random silly thought, a conversation, or a song. In my normal day to day life, listening to music would often give me a lovely big wonky earworm. I would send these out to the world, and sometimes they got a good response. The misheard lyric became a recurring @trouteyes feature. We all get the words of songs inside out, back to front, or upside down, so it feels pretty universal. As time went on, I found I had amassed zillions of them and a nice man called Joel suggested they could form the basis of something called a book – whatever the heck that is!

So here they are, loads of them, all together in paper form, to be enjoyed in all their silliness. I really hope that they give you a strong amount of nice feelings.

Very best swishes to you all

@trouteyes
Captain of the Good Team

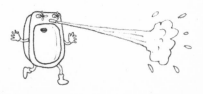

Last night a bidet
drenched my wife.

And you may find yourself behind the wheel of a large avocado mobile.

Boom boom boom let me hear
you say Wales.

I've reason to believe we all will be received in Poundland. Poundland.

And we rely on each other.
hee-haw. From one donkey to
another, hee-haw.

Pre-Raphaelite girls go around the outside. Around the outside. Around the outside.

Too shy, shy long conk

gammy eye.

I'm waiting for my Nan.

26 Bensons in my hand.

I can tweet @Deirdre now
@Lorraine has gone.

'There ain't no party like
an S Club party'
– Lemmy

And then I go and spoil it all
by buying something stupid like
Dutch tofu.

Almonds are a girl's best friend.

Bum licky you're so slime, you're so slime, you blow my mind, bum licky, bum licky.

Polly put Def Leppard on.

Leppard on. Leppard on.

Polly put Def Leppard on

we'll all have tea.

Mild thing. You make my
heart sing. You make everything
pleasant. Mild thing, I think I'm
fond of you.

If I said you had a beautiful
Brompton would you fold it
against me?

You were working

as a racist in a hostile bra,

when I met you.

He knows when you are Lupin.

He knows when you are Snape.

Six o'clock already I was just
in the middle of a dream. I was
kissing Danny DeVito by a crystal
blue Italian stream.

Look for a Claire's Accessories

a simple Claire's Accessories.

I was looking for some action
and all I found were cygnets and
a waterfall.

You took a mystery and made Fred want it. You took a pedestal and put Daphne on it.

What's that nose coming
over the hill, is it a long conk?
Is it a long conk?

All that she wants is a bit of baccy,
she's going to get some.

Robert the weirdo's waiting.

Talking in Vulcan.

Talking in Vulcan.

68 gnus will never die.

68 gnus our battle cry.

Love and marriage. Love and marriage. They go together like egg and cabbage.

Giant steps are what you take,
farting on the moon.

Sedaka. Sudoku. Sudoku. Sedaka.
Let's call the Neil thing maths.

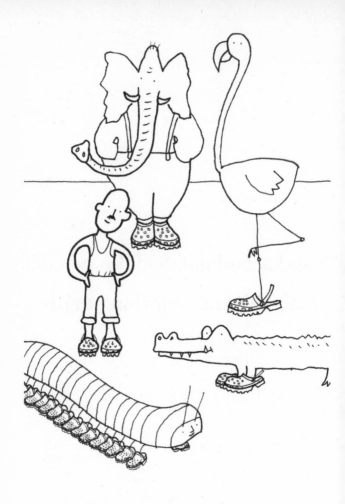

Comfy, comfy, comfy Crocs
of rubber.

When the feeling's right,

I'm gonna run all night,

I'm gonna run Peru.

BACK once again with the
Renegade Master
(we've been to Relate and we've
decided to give it another go).

I get locked out, but I get in
again, you're never gonna lock
me out, I get locked out but I
get in again you're never gonna
lock me out.

Couscous for me, save all your
couscous for me.

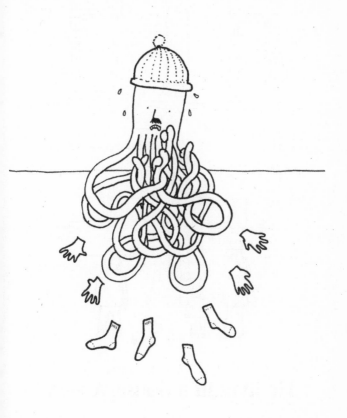

If you're anxious and you know it
clasp your hands.

He lives in a house. A very
small house. He's a sentry. He
lives in a house. A very small
house. He's a sentry.

How do you like your eggs in the morning? I like mine with a fist.

Love me for a reason and let the
reason be girth.

Mary had some Lidl lamb, it's price was nice and low.

YOUR OWN
PERSONAL
JUDITH

It was only a Winter Sale. Just another Winter Sale and why should the world take note of another load of shit that failed?

We were born within an hour of each other. Our mothers said we could be sister and brother. Your name was Federer. Federer.

Let's get quizzical. Quizzical.
I wanna get quizzical. Let's get
into quizzical.

When I get that feeling I need

saxophone cleaning.

All we hear is Lady O'Gaga.

Lady O'Googoo.

Are you going to Scarborough Fair? No mate, sounds shit.

Dope. A deer. A female deer. Yay.

A drop of golden sun.

Ain't no stoppin' us now.

We're in the nude.

Hit me with your memory stick.

Three nice Jpegs click, click, click.

Guinea, Guinea, Guinea a pig
after midnight.

Don't like the way you twerk it.

No dignity.

Depeche Mode! What's it like in Perthshire?

It's a lot

It's a lot

It's a lot

It's a lot

It's a lot

It's a lot

It's a lot like Fife.

My father was a gambolling lamb,

down in Milton Keynes.

Every bothy yurts. Sometimes.

By the look in your eye,

I can see you have a stye,

is it lack of sleep?

When I met you in the
restaurant. You could tell I had
a lengthy conk.

I bet that you look cack on the dance floor, dancing like a dickhead from 1924 yeah from 1924.

She bought an itsy bitsy teenie weenie little jar of light tahini.

We got stars directing our fate and we're praying it's not too late, Fungruntium.

If you don't Naomi by now. You
will never never never Naomi.

If you go down to the fridge
today you're sure of a big surprise.
Today's the day the teddy bears
have their shit nicked.

Wake me up before you go go.

I am planning on going solo.

Heavy rain is in my ears and
in my eyes.

Tumble out of bed and stumble
on a pigeon, pour myself a cup
of ambition.

I'm gonna put on an iron shirt

and chase Kenny out my yurt.

You can ring my Muuuuuuuum

My Mum. Ring my Mum.

You can ring my Muuuuuuuum.

YOU. MAKE. ME. FEEL. LIKE. A.
NATURAL SALMON.

Oh, I wanna dance with
some chutney.
I wanna feel the heat with
some chutney.
Yeah, I wanna dance with
some chutney.
With some chutney who loves me.

It's selfie time and there's no need
to be afraid. At selfie time we let
in light and we banish shade.

Sign your name across my conk,

I want you to be my Bernard.

Prince Charming. Prince Charming. Stop calling Mandy, pretending to be Jason.

We're up all night to smoke baccy.

We're up all night to smoke baccy.

We're up all night to smoke baccy.

Remember Chumbawumba.

Remember Chumbawumba.

Remember member member

Chumba Wumba Wumba

Wumba tonight.

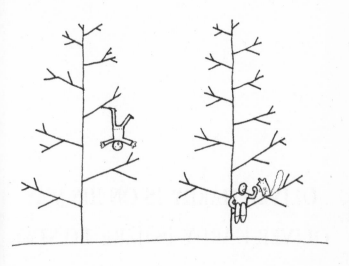

When you needed a neighbour,

I was next door. I was next door.

When you NEEDED a neighbour

I was next door.

OLIVER HARDY IS ON HIS WAY.

OLIVER HARDY IS HERE TO STAY.

He's a thin bald wizard.

I didn't know I was looking for
love. I didn't know I was looking
for love until cheese fondue
fondue fondue fondue.

Live those dreams.

Scheme those schemes.

Got to hit me (hit me)

Hit me (hit me)

Hit me with red kidney beans

(Ow, ow, ow).

The Who let the Mods out.

The Who. Who.

He's a sleazy bugger. He'll piss
you off when you don't need it.

Specs and rugs and sausage rolls,

are all my mind and body needs.

Relax, don't do it, when you
wanna fax Judith.

Song Index

Page 11

Last night a bidet drenched my wife.

Last Night a DJ Saved My Life - Indeep

Page 12

And you may find yourself behind the wheel of a large avocado mobile.

Once in a Lifetime - Talking Heads

Page 13

Boom Boom Boom let me hear you say Wales.

Boom Boom Boom - The Outhere Brothers

Page 14

I've reason to believe we all will be received in
 Poundland. Poundland.

Graceland - Paul Simon

Page 15

And we rely on each other, hee-haw. From one donkey
 to another, hee-haw.

**Islands in the Stream - Dolly Parton and Kenny
 Rogers**

Page 16

Pre-Raphaelite girls go around the outside. Around the
 outside. Around the outside.

Buffalo Gals - Malcolm McLaren

Page 17

Too shy shy, long conk gammy eye.

Too Shy - Kajagoogoo

Page 18

I'm waiting for my Nan. 26 Bensons in my hand.

I'm Waiting for the Man - The Velvet Underground

Page 19

I can tweet @Deirdre now @Lorraine has gone.

I Can See Clearly Now - Jimmy Cliff

Page 20
'There ain't no party like an S Club party.' Lemmy
S Club Party - S Club 7

Page 21
And then I go and spoil it all by buying something stupid
    like Dutch tofu.
Somethin Stupid - Frank Sinatra

Page 22
Almonds are a girl's best friend
Diamonds are a Girl's Best Friend - Marilyn Monroe

Page 23
Bum licky you're so slime, you're so slime, you blow my
    mind, bum licky, bum licky.
Mickey - Toni Basil

Page 24
Polly put Def Leppard on. Leppard on. Leppard on.
    Polly put Def Leppard on we'll all have tea.
Polly Put the Kettle on

Page 25
Mild thing. You make my heart sing. You make
    everything pleasant. Mild thing, I think I'm fond of
    you.
Wild Thing - The Troggs

Page 26
If I said you had a beautiful Brompton would you fold it
   against me?
If I Said You Had a Beautiful Body - Dr Hook

Page 27
You were working as a racist in a hostile bra when I
   met you
Don't You Want Me? - The Human League

Page 28
He knows when you are Lupin. He knows when you are
   Snape.
Santa Claus is Comin to Town - Mariah Carey

Page 29
Six o'clock already I was just in the middle of a dream.
   I was kissing Danny DeVito by a crystal blue Italian
   stream.
Manic Monday - The Bangles

Page 30
Look for a Claire's Accessories a simple Claire's
   Accessories.
The Bare Necessities (The Jungle Book)

Page 31

I was loooking for some action and all I found were
  cygnets and a waterfall.
Cigarettes and Alcohol - Oasis

Page 32

You took a mystery and made Fred want it. You took a
  pedestal and put Daphne on it.
Chain Reaction - Diana Ross

Page 33

What's that nose coming over the hill, is it a long conk?
  Is it a long conk?
Monster - The Automatic

Page 34

All that she wants is a bit of baccy.
All That She Wants - Ace of Base

Page 35

Robert the weirdo's waiting. Talking in Vulcan. Talking
  in Vulcan.
Robert De Niro's Waiting - Bananarama

Page 36

68 gnus will never die. 68 gnus our battle cry.
68 Guns - The Alarm

Page 37

Love and marriage. Love and marriage. They go
together, like egg and cabbage.
Love and Marriage - Frank Sinatra

Page 38

Giant steps are what you take, farting on the moon.
Walking on the Moon - The Police

Page 39

Sedaka. Sudoku. Sudoku. Sedaka. Let's call the Neil
thing maths.
Let's Call the Whole Thing Off - Ella Fitzgerald

Page 40

Comfy, comfy, comfy Crocs of rubber.
Venus in Furs - The Velvet Underground

Page 42

BACK once again with the Renegade Master.
We've been to Relate and we've decided to give it
another go.
Renegade Master - Wildchild

Page 43

I get locked out but I get in again, You're never gonna
lock me out, I get locked out but I get in again, You're
never gonna lock me out
Tubthumping - Chumbawamba

Page 44
Couscous for me, save all your couscous for me
Save All Your Kisses For Me - Brotherhood of Man

Page 45
If you're anxious and you know it clasp your hands.
If You're Happy and You Know It

Page 46
He lives in a house. A very small house. He's a sentry. He
  lives in a house. A very small house. He's a sentry.
Country House - Blur

Page 47
How do you like your eggs in the morning?
  I like mine with a fist.
How Do You Like Your Eggs in the Morning?
  Dean Martin and Helen O'Connell

Page 48
Love me for a reason and let the reason be girth.
Love Me for a Reason - Boyzone

Page 49
Mary had some Lidl lamb it's price was nice and low.
Mary Had a Little Lamb

Page 50
YOUR OWN PERSONAL JUDITH
Personal Jesus - Depeche Mode

Page 51
It was only a Winter Sale. Just another Winter Sale and
  why should the world take note of another load of shit
  that failed?
A Winter's Tale - David Essex

Page 52
We were born within an hour of each other. Our
  mothers said we could be sister and brother. Your
  name was Federer. Federer.
Disco 2000 - Pulp

Page 53
Let's get quizzical. Quizzical. I wanna get quizzical. Let's
  get into quizzical.
Physical - Olivia Newton -John

Page 54
When I get that feeling I need saxophone cleaning.
Sexual Healing - Marvin Gaye

Page 55
All we hear is Lady O'Gaga. Lady O'Googo.
Radio Ga Ga - Queen

Page 56

Are you going to Scarborough Fair? No mate, sounds shit.

Scarborough Fair - Simon and Garfunkel

Page 57

Dope. A deer. A female deer. Yay. A drop of golden sun.

Do Re Mi - The Sound of Music

Page 58

Ain't no stoppin us now. We're in the nude.

Ain't No Stoppin Us Now - Mcfadden and Whitehead

Page 59

Hit me with your memory stick. Three nice Jpegs click, click, click.

Hit me with your Rhythm Stick - Ian Dury and the Blockheads

Page 60

Guinea, Guinea, Guinea, a pig after midnight.

Gimme Gimme Gimme (A Man After Midnight) - Abba

Page 61

Don't like the way you twerk it. No dignity.

No Diggity - Blackstreet Ft Dr Dre and Queen Pen

Page 62 / 63
Depeche Mode! What's it like in Perthshire?

It's a lot

It's a lot

It's a lot

It's a lot

It's a lot

It's a lot

It's a lot like Fife

Master and Servant - Depeche Mode

Page 64
My father was a gambolling lamb, down in Milton
Keynes.

House of the Rising Sun - The Animals

Page 65
Every bothy yurts. Sometimes.

Everybody Hurts - REM

Page 66
By the look in your eye, I can see you have a stye, is it lack
of sleep?

Wherever I Lay My Hat - Marvin Gaye

Page 67
When I met you in the restaurant. You could tell I had a
lengthy conk.

Dreaming - Blondie

Page 68

I bet that you look cack on the dance floor, dancing like a
dickhead from 1924 yeah from 1924

**I Bet You Look Good On The Dancefloor - The Arctic
Monkeys**

Page 69

She bought an itsy bitsy teenie weenie little jar of light
tahini.

**Itsy Bitsy Teenie Weenie Yellow Polka Dot Bikini -
Bryan Hyland**

Page70

We got stars directing our fate and we're preying it's not
too late, Fungruntium.

Millenium - Robbie Williams

Page 71

If you don't Naomi by now. You will never never Naomi.

If You Don't Know Me – Simply Red

Page 72

If you go down to the fridge today you're sure of a big
surprise

Today's the day the teddy bears have their shit nicked.

Teddy Bears Picnic

Page 73

Wake me up before you go go. I am planning on going
    solo.

Wake Me Up Before You Go Go - Wham!

Page 74

Heavy rain is in my ears and in my eyes.

Penny Lane - The Beatles

Page 75

Tumble out of bed and stumble on a pigeon pour myself
    a cup of ambition.

9-5 - Dolly Parton

Page 76

I'm gonna put on an iron shirt and chase Kenny out
    my yurt.

I Chase The Devil - Max Romeo and the Upsetters.

Page 77

You can ring my Muuuuuuuum

My Mum. Ring my Mum.

You can ring my Muuuuuuuum.

Ring my Bell - Anita Ward

YOU. MAKE. ME. FEEL. LIKE. A. NATURAL
SALMON.

**(You Make Me Feel Like) A Natural Woman - Aretha
Franklin**

Oh, I wanna dance with some chutney. I wanna feel the
heat with some chutney. Yeah, I wanna dance with
some chutney. With some chutney who loves me.

With Somebody Who Loves Me -Whitney Houston

It's selfie time and there's no need to be afraid. At selfie
time we let in light and we banish shade.

Do They Know it's Christmas? - Band Aid

Sign your name across my conk, I want you to be my
Bernard.

Sign Your Name - Terence Trent D'Arby

Prince Charming. Prince Charming. Stop calling
Mandy's pretending you are Jason.

Prince Charming - Adam and the Ants

Page 83

We're up all night to smoke baccy, we're up all night to smoke baccy, we're up all night to smoke baccy.

Get Lucky - Daft Punk

Page 84

Remember Chumbawumba. Remember Chumbawumba. Remember member member Chumba Wumba Wumba Wumba tonight.

Remember you're a Womble - The Wombles

Page 85

When you needed a neighbour, I was next door. I was next door. When you NEEDED a neighbour I was next door.

When I Needed a Neighbour

Page 86

OLIVER HARDY IS ON HIS WAY. OLIVER HARDY IS HERE TO STAY.

Oliver's Army - Elvis Costello and the Attractions

Page 87

He's a thin bald wizard.

Pinball Wizard - The Who

Page 88

I didn't know I was looking for love.

I didn't know I was looking for love until cheese fondue
fondue fondue fondue

**I didn't Know I was Looking For Love - Everything but
the Girl**

Page 89

Live those dreams. Scheme those schemes. Got to hit me
(hit me) Hit me (hit me) Hit me with red kidney beans
(Ow, ow, ow).

Relax - Frankie Goes to Hollywood

Page 90

The Who let the Mods out. The Who. Who.

Who Let the Dogs Out? - Baha Men

Page 91

He's a sleazy bugger. He'll piss you off when you don't
need it.

Easy Lover - Phil Collins

Page 92

Specs and rugs and sausage rolls, are all my mind and
body needs.

**Sex & Drugs & Rock & Roll - Ian Dury and the
Blockheads**

Relax, don't do it, when you want to fax Judith.

Relax – Frankie Goes to Hollywood